WWI

AIRCRAFT OF WORLD WAR I

JOHN HAMILTON

VISIT US AT
WWW.ABDOPUB.COM

Published by ABDO & Daughters, an imprint of ABDO Publishing Company, 4940 Viking Drive, Suite 622, Edina, Minnesota 55435. Copyright ©2004 by Abdo Consulting Group, Inc. International copyrights reserved in all countries. No part of this book may be reproduced in any form without written permission from the publisher.

Printed in the United States.

Edited by Tamara L. Britton
Graphic Design: John Hamilton
Cover Design: Mighty Media
Photos and illustrations:
    Thomas Genth, p. 7, 8, 10, 19, 21
    Holcomb's Aerodrome, p. 7
    Mark Miller, p. 1, 4-5, 9, 11, 12-13, 15, 16, 17, 18, 26
    National Archives, p. 8, 10, 11, 22, 23, 24, 25, 28, 29
    Rosebud's WWI Aviation Image Archive, p. 10, 14, 15, 20, 21, 27
    Wright Brothers Aeroplane Company and Museum of Pioneer Aviation, p. 6
    Cover photo: Corbis

Library of Congress Cataloging-in-Publication Data

Hamilton, John, 1959-
    Aircraft of World War I / John Hamilton.
    p. cm.—(World War I)
    Includes index.
    Summary: An overview of the use of aircraft in World War I.
    ISBN 1-57765-912-0
    1. Airplanes, Military—Juvenile literature. 2. World War, 1914-1918—Equipment and supplies—Juvenile literature. [1. Airplanes, Military. 2. World War, 1914-1918—Equipment and supplies.] I. Title.

D522.7 .H33 2003
940.4'4—dc21

2002033294

TABLE OF CONTENTS

KNIGHTS OF THE SKY

SOLDIERS WHO WERE STUCK in the trenches of World War I fought a new kind of war. Instead of facing the enemy and outsmarting him on the battlefield, troops took cover in muddy pits. Artillery shells rained down, launched by an unseen enemy, sometimes from miles away. Machine guns and hidden snipers mowed down anyone daring or foolish enough to venture out into no-man's-land—the killing fields between the trenches.

Neither side was used to fighting this way. World War I lasted for years, cost millions of lives, and yet little ground was won until the very end of the war. It was a war of attrition, where each side hoped for victory by holding out the longest. Men were so thoughtlessly sent to their deaths that the battlefield became known as a meat grinder. Honor and heroism didn't seem to have a place in this new, modern kind of war.

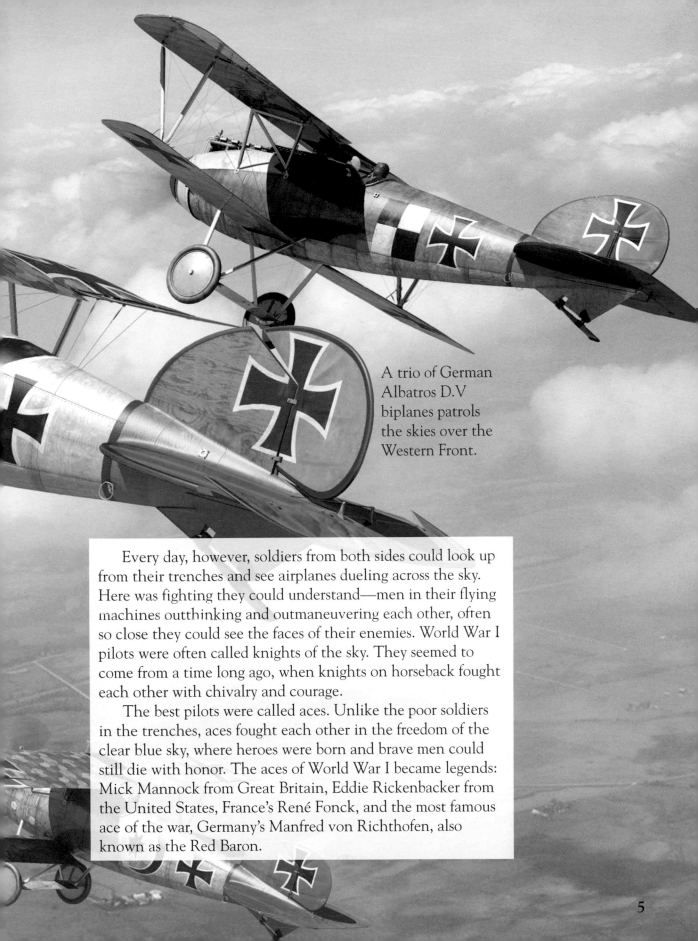

A trio of German Albatros D.V biplanes patrols the skies over the Western Front.

Every day, however, soldiers from both sides could look up from their trenches and see airplanes dueling across the sky. Here was fighting they could understand—men in their flying machines outthinking and outmaneuvering each other, often so close they could see the faces of their enemies. World War I pilots were often called knights of the sky. They seemed to come from a time long ago, when knights on horseback fought each other with chivalry and courage.

The best pilots were called aces. Unlike the poor soldiers in the trenches, aces fought each other in the freedom of the clear blue sky, where heroes were born and brave men could still die with honor. The aces of World War I became legends: Mick Mannock from Great Britain, Eddie Rickenbacker from the United States, France's René Fonck, and the most famous ace of the war, Germany's Manfred von Richthofen, also known as the Red Baron.

EARLY AIRCRAFT

"We do not consider that aeroplanes will be of any possible use for war purposes."
Richard Haldane, British Secretary of State for War, 1910

WHEN FIGHTING BROKE OUT in World War I, powered aircraft had been flying for barely 10 years. On December 17, 1903, Orville and Wilbur Wright flew their first plane, *Flyer 1*, at Kitty Hawk, North Carolina. The first flight lasted 12 seconds, and achieved an astonishing distance of 120 feet (37 m). Within five years the brothers had developed a military version of their airplane that could stay aloft for more than an hour and reach speeds of more than 40 miles (64 km) per hour. The United States Army ordered airplanes from the Wrights, but eventually lost interest in the program. The Army couldn't decide how best to use flying machines on the battlefield.

Above: Orville Wright pilots a 1909 Wright Military Flyer over Fort Meyer, Virginia.

While the U.S. military dragged its feet, aircraft development continued, especially in France, Great Britain, and Germany. But even in these countries, people in the armed forces could scarcely understand how important the airplane would eventually become. Marshall Ferdinand Foch, commander in chief of the Allied forces during World War I, once said, "The aircraft is all very well for sport, but for the army it is useless."

The history of successful manned flight began in 1783, when two French inventors, the Montgolfier brothers, demonstrated a balloon sturdy enough to achieve the first free flight by humans. One hundred years later, balloons were used by the Union Army to observe Confederate forces during the American Civil War. Throughout the nineteenth century, inventors worked hard to perfect gliders.

During the late 1800s, early aviators began work on powered flight. They wanted to build a flying machine that was powered by an engine. Then the pilot could choose the direction of the craft, instead of being at the mercy of the wind. However, the steam engines of the time were too heavy to put on an airplane. By 1903, the Wright brothers mounted a lighter-weight gasoline engine on their bi-winged plane and made history.

By the time World War I started in August of 1914, airplanes were still relatively primitive in design. They were slow, underpowered, and unarmed. The French Bleriot XI was a fragile plane with a weak engine that often broke down. Nevertheless, it was the first plane to cross the English Channel, in 1909. The Bleriot was also the first plane to go to war, when Italian forces fought Turkey in 1911. French and British forces used planes of this type in 1914 and 1915, until planes with more powerful engines were developed.

Most of the airplanes of World War I, even the advanced models that flew toward the end of the war, were simple machines with skeletons made of wood or aluminum. The frames were wrapped in silk or linen covered in varnish, which easily caught fire.

The planes' simplicity sometimes made them difficult to shoot down. Bullets often passed harmlessly through the thin fabric skin. Still, piloting a World War I airplane was hazardous duty. If enemy bullets struck gas tanks, the planes went down in flames. Another common hazard occurred when planes went into steep dives. As the wind roared by during these high-speed maneuvers, the wings were sometimes torn right off the fuselage.

As airplane technology became more advanced, planes were made sturdier and more dependable. But it was still extremely dangerous being a World War I pilot. The average life expectancy of a pilot on the Western Front was only three weeks.

Above: A Bleriot XI (upper plane) comes in for a landing at a French airshow. *Below:* German soldiers inspect the wreckage of a Junkers J1 ground attack airplane.

SCOUTS

WHEN THE WAR began in August 1914, Germany had the largest air service, even though it included only 232 aircraft. Great Britain had 113 aircraft, and France had 138. But as the war progressed, each country would produce airplanes by the thousands.

At the beginning of the war, airplanes were used mainly to find the location of enemy troops on the ground. This job, which is called *reconnaissance*, was very important so that artillery fire could be directed more accurately at the enemy. Planes could also easily spot when large masses of enemy troops were moving into position to launch an attack.

Above: An American observer operates a Graflex camera.
Right: German aviator Erich Priese
Below: A crater-filled battlefield photographed from an Allied reconnaissance airplane

In the past, cavalry was used for reconnaissance. But during World War I, men on horses were easy targets for long-range snipers. Also, on the Western Front, horses had a difficult time traveling through the maze of muddy trenches and barbed wire. Airplanes, with their freedom of movement,

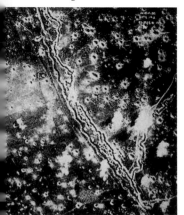

quickly became an important replacement for the cavalry. When the weather was good, pilots could easily spot the enemy and take photographs for the war planners on the ground to study.

At the beginning of World War I, airplanes weren't seriously considered to be weapons of destruction. The first planes used in the war were called "scouts," a name that stuck even into the later years of the war, when airplanes were used as fighters and bombers. From the beginning, pilots had been dropping small handheld bombs on enemy troops and buildings. Soon they began to arm themselves against enemy planes as well.

During the first months of the war, unarmed planes went up to search for enemy troop positions. When they passed each other in the air, opposing pilots often smiled and waved to each other. This friendliness didn't last long, however. Pilots quickly realized that the information the enemy was gathering was hurting their comrades on the ground. Whoever controlled the sky had a very big advantage on the battlefield.

Above: A German Albatros D.V on patrol over the Western Front

Above: German and French aviators shoot at each other with pistols during a raid over Paris, France.

Aircrews began throwing heavy objects like bricks at enemy planes. They also shot at them with shotguns or pistols. Machine guns soon appeared on two-seater planes so that passengers, whose main job was to spot the enemy on the ground, could also shoot at enemy planes.

Troops on the ground fired at enemy airplanes, but the planes were usually flying too fast or too high to be hit. Antiaircraft guns were developed that fired shells that exploded in mid-air, sending jagged pieces of metal, called *shrapnel*, in all directions. Antiaircraft weapons, known as *Archie*, weren't very accurate during World War I. Many soldiers complained that shrapnel falling back to earth was more dangerous to them than to the airplanes being fired at.

Sometimes, though, Archie hit its target. British flyer Arthur Gould Lee was fighting German planes during the Battle of Cambrai in November 1917 when his plane's engine was hit by shrapnel. He glided safely to the ground, then watched as more planes were hit by antiaircraft guns. He later wrote, "I saw something I'd never seen before… A machine was hit by a shell and blown to fragments. Bits of it fell quickly, like the engine and pilot's body, but most of it seemed to float down lazily like leaves from trees in autumn."

Above: An Allied pilot drops a handheld bomb over the side of his airplane.
Right: This photo of an Albatros in flight was taken by German aviator Adolph Genth.

Above: An interior view of an Albatros D.V cockpit, with seat removed
Left: An American antiaircraft gun crew scans the skies for enemy planes.

ANATOMY OF AN ALBATROS D.V

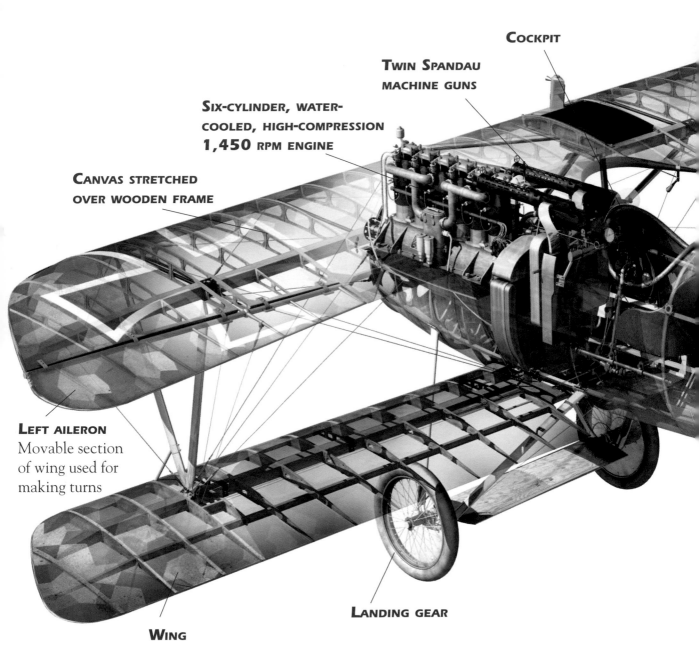

COCKPIT

TWIN SPANDAU
MACHINE GUNS

SIX-CYLINDER, WATER-
COOLED, HIGH-COMPRESSION
1,450 RPM ENGINE

CANVAS STRETCHED
OVER WOODEN FRAME

LEFT AILERON
Movable section
of wing used for
making turns

LANDING GEAR

WING

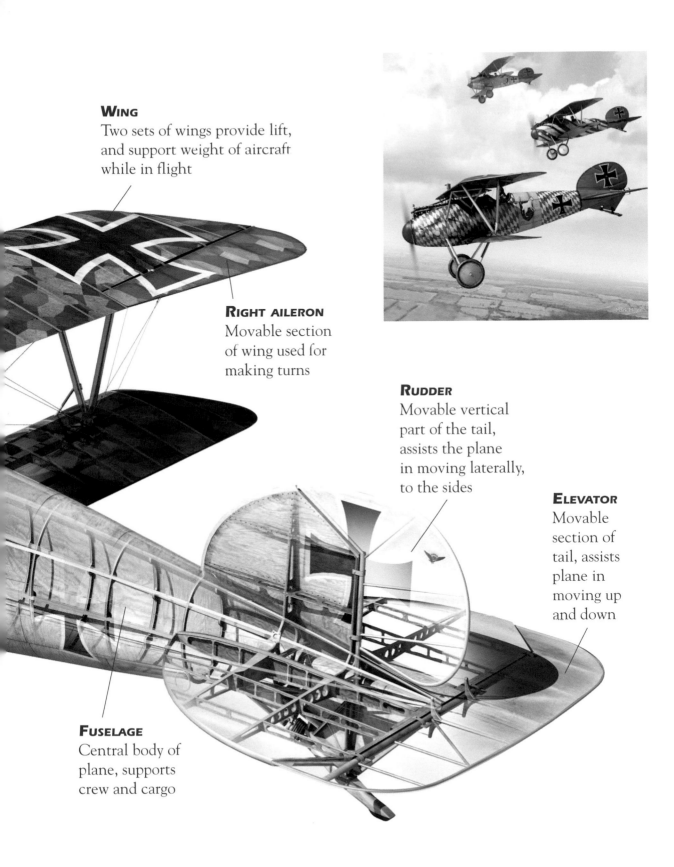

WING
Two sets of wings provide lift, and support weight of aircraft while in flight

RIGHT AILERON
Movable section of wing used for making turns

RUDDER
Movable vertical part of the tail, assists the plane in moving laterally, to the sides

ELEVATOR
Movable section of tail, assists plane in moving up and down

FUSELAGE
Central body of plane, supports crew and cargo

THE FOKKER SCOURGE

ALTHOUGH ANTIAIRCRAFT GUNS were sometimes effective, both sides realized they needed to develop planes whose main job was to shoot down the enemy. These specialized fighter planes were sturdier, and fitted with more powerful engines.

Above: Anthony Fokker in the cockpit of his EIII Eindecker

An important development in making fighter planes was putting machine guns on the front. This made it much easier for pilots to shoot down the enemy. The biggest problem was finding a way to shoot bullets through the whirling propeller blades.

A year before the war started, German inventor Franz Schneider created a device that made a machine gun fire only after a propeller blade had passed safely by. The device was called an *interrupter mechanism*. The German military showed little interest in Schneider's invention, and failed to incorporate it into their aircraft.

Meanwhile, in France, Raymond Saulnier also tried to invent an interrupter mechanism, but couldn't get it to work properly. In frustration, he wrapped sheets of metal around the edge of the propeller's blades, which deflected any stray bullets that weren't perfectly synchronized. The system worked, but it was crude and not very accurate. In 1914, French pilot Roland Garros, who was using the deflector system on his plane, crashed behind enemy lines. The German military took the deflector propeller and gave it to their brilliant Dutch aircraft designer Anthony Fokker.

Fokker didn't like the deflector design, and worked instead to perfect a practical synchronizing mechanism that would fire the machine gun only when the propeller blade wasn't in the line of fire. In May of 1915, he put the new device on his latest plane design, the Fokker EIII monoplane. The EIII, also called the Eindecker, was fitted with two of Fokker's synchronized machine guns. It instantly became a fearsome weapon in the hands of skilled pilots, easily outclassing enemy planes like the British Bristol Scout D or the French Morane Type N.

The "Fokker Scourge" over the Western Front lasted through the end of 1915 and into the following year. Until then, the Germans ruled the skies.

Above: Anthony Fokker (left) tests his synchronizing mechanism.

Above: A poster advertising the Fokker factory in Schwerin, Germany
Right: A pair of Spandau machine guns mounted in front of the cockpit of an Albatros D.V.

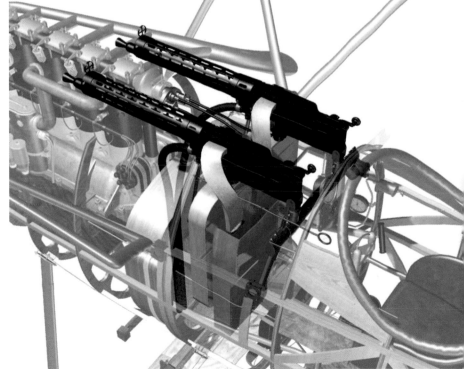

DOGFIGHTS

Above: A German biplane goes down in flames.
Facing page: A pair of German Albatros D.V's chases a British Sopwith Camel.
Below: A Sopwith Camel rests in an airfield.

BY THE END OF 1915, British and French designers came up with airplanes that matched the dreaded German Eindecker. The French Nieuport and British De Havilland 2 were faster and more maneuverable than earlier planes. And by mid-1916, Allied planes were fitted with machine-gun synchronizers of their own.

Throughout the remaining years of the war, each side raced to invent sturdier planes that could fly higher and faster, and had better weapons. As the war years dragged on, planes entered the field of battle that would go down in history. The Germans rolled out the Albatros D.V, and the Fokker Dr. I triplane. The Fokker D.VII biplane was considered by many pilots to be the best overall fighter of the war. The British developed the Sopwith Pup and the Sopwith Camel, while the French produced the Nieuport 17, the Spad 7, and Spad 13. Many other planes—some good, some truly terrible in design—entered service during the war.

Mark W. Miller 2002

Above: German Albatros D.V's on patrol, looking for a dogfight with Allied planes.

Fighter planes dueled over the battlefields, making acrobatic turns and shooting at each other in what became known as dogfights. Sometimes whole squadrons of planes would fight, with dozens of planes dodging in and out of a tight airspace while shooting at each other. A German unit led by Manfred von Richthofen, the Red Baron, was so skilled at flying in combat that Allied airmen called it the Flying Circus.

Flying in airplanes was so new in World War I that combat techniques had to be learned in battle. German ace Oswald Boelcke led the first squadron, or *Jagdstaffel*, whose main job was to find and shoot down enemy planes. (*Jagdstaffel* is German for "hunting group.") Boelcke was a great pilot who soon developed basic rules of air combat. These rules included keeping the sun behind you to blind the enemy, always carrying through with an attack once you've started it, and firing only at close range when your target is within your sights. The Allies came up with tactics of their own, including hiding in clouds and only attacking in superior numbers.

A favorite tactic was to dive on the enemy from above and hold fire until the target was very close. This took steely nerves because if a pilot shot too soon, not only would he probably miss, he would also alert the enemy to his presence and ruin the element of surprise. The early rules of combat weren't too complicated. As Boelcke once said, "Well, it is quite simple. I fly close to my man, aim well and then he falls down."

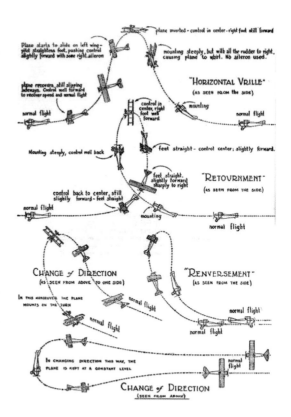

Above: A page from American ace Eddie Rickenbacker's WWI memoirs
Left: German ace Oswald Boelcke climbs into his Fokker Eindecker

ZEPPELINS

LIGHTER-THAN-AIR TECHNOLOGY had been developed years before World War I began. Unlike airplanes, blimps and airships were sturdy and could lift several tons of equipment, including bombs to attack enemy targets on the ground.

Germany was the leader in airship development. The Zeppelin Company built gigantic machines that inspired awe as they passed overhead. Count Ferdinand von Zeppelin invented powered airships in 1900. Zeppelins, as most airships came to be known, were huge, slow-moving machines with rigid, internal frames. During the war they sometimes measured more than 400 feet (122 m) long. These giant airships were filled with buoyant—and extremely flammable—hydrogen gas.

Above: Zeppelin L70 is prepared for a mission
Right: Ferdinand von Zeppelin awaits the arrival of one of his airships in Leipzig, Germany.
Below: A pair of Zeppelins are maintained in a German hanger.

Great Britain was first attacked by German airships in the spring of 1915. Germany was determined to disrupt English war factories, hoping this would shorten the war.

Zeppelin in Erwartung seines Luftschiffes in Leipzig.

At the beginning of World War I, Zeppelins could fly higher than airplanes. The first Zeppelins to bomb Great Britain crossed the English Channel on calm, moonlit nights with little fear of being shot down.

The German bombing campaign didn't really affect the outcome of the war, but it inspired terror among the British population. Many people had never even seen an airplane before. The sight of a giant Zeppelin lumbering across the night sky and dropping bombs on cities caused great panic. This was especially true in London, one of the prime targets of German bombing. In all, there were more than 50 Zeppelin raids on Great Britain. Approximately 557 people were killed, and another 1,358 were wounded.

As the war progressed, the Allies developed airplanes with engines powerful enough to fly as high as the Zeppelins. Allied aircraft shot special incendiary bullets at the slow-moving airships. These ignited the Zeppelin's hydrogen gas and created huge fireballs, which the Allied pilots had to be careful to avoid.

As more and more Zeppelins were shot down, Germany gradually stopped using them to bomb Great Britain. By the end of 1917, it was too dangerous to fly airships over enemy territory. Instead, airships and balloons were used through the remainder of the war as observation platforms for directing artillery, and especially for spotting submarines.

Above top: A Zeppelin conducts a nighttime raid. *Above:* The twisted metal frame is all that remains of a Zeppelin after crashing to Earth. *Left:* When Zeppelins became too vulnerable for bombing missions, Germany relied on the Gotha, a long-range bomber airplane. Great Britain had its own bomber, the Handley Page H.P. 0/100, like the captured one shown here at a German airfield.

ACES

HIGHLY SKILLED AVIATORS sometimes shot down dozens of enemy planes. These were the aces of World War I, brave and daring men whose very name made enemy pilots tremble.

The term "ace" first appeared in French newspapers in 1915. It was used to describe Adolphe Pegoud after he became the first pilot to shoot down five German aircraft. French aerial units began publishing the scores of pilots—the number of enemy aircraft they had shot down.

Germany also started keeping track of its pilots' air victories, but they had to shoot down eight airplanes (later 16) before they became aces. The British and Americans followed the French example, giving their pilots the title of ace after five confirmed victories.

Only five percent of World War I pilots achieved the status of ace. They became celebrities in their home countries. Regular soldiers, stranded in the mud of the Western Front, greatly admired the aces, and were eager to read of their adventures high above in the clear blue sky.

Below: An American aviator stationed in France poses with his airplane.

22

RENÉ FONCK, FRANCE

René Fonck was the highest scoring French ace of World War I, scoring 75 kills. He claimed to have shot down 127 enemy aircraft, but only 75 could be verified and entered into the record books.

Above: French ace René Fonck next to his Spad 12

Fonck was a gifted pilot whose favorite tactic was to fly very close to the enemy before firing. He often shot down the enemy on the first try this way. Fonck said, "I put my bullets into the target as if I placed them there by hand." On two separate occasions, Fonck shot down six Germans in one day.

Unlike most aces, Fonck survived the war. He would have been a popular national hero, but his personality was very irritating, and he could be a show-off. A friend once said of Fonck, "He is a tiresome braggart and even a bore, but in the air, a slashing rapier, a steel blade tempered with unblemished courage and priceless skill…"

EDWARD MANNOCK, GREAT BRITAIN

Edward "Mick" Mannock scored 73 victories in World War I, the third highest after Germany's Manfred von Richthofen and France's René Fonck. Mannock joined the British air services in 1916, at a time when war in the air was going through a transition. No longer a dashing, chivalrous pastime, air war became more and more ruthless as pilots concentrated on shooting down the enemy.

In 1914, Turkey joined the Central Powers, aligning itself with Germany and Austria-Hungary. Mannock had been in the country working for a British telephone company. He was thrown into prison, where he was abused and maltreated. On the verge of death, he was finally sent home to England.

Below: Edward "Mick" Mannock

Perhaps because of his mistreatment in prison, Mannock despised the Germans, especially when he read of atrocities committed against Belgian civilians. Mannock's rage drove him to shoot down as many German planes as possible. By the end of 1917, he had already scored 23 victories. Mannock showed no mercy in the air. He once said, "The swines are better dead—no prisoners!"

Mannock had great piloting skills. He was also much admired by the men who served under him. Many considered him the best flight leader of the war. German aircraft never once surprised his flights.

Mannock died in July 1918. He was flying low after following one of his victims to watch him crash. Someone on the ground shot and struck Mannock's fuel tank. The plane burst into flames and nosedived into no-man's-land. His body was found by the Germans, but was never recovered by the Allies. It is unknown where he was buried.

A year after his death, Mannock was posthumously awarded the Victoria Cross, Britain's highest military award for bravery. During the ceremony, Mannock was called "an outstanding example of fearless courage, remarkable skill, devotion to duty and self-sacrifice, which has never been surpassed."

EDDIE RICKENBACKER, UNITED STATES

Below: Eddie Rickenbacker in his Spad in France.

Edward "Eddie" Rickenbacker was a professional racecar driver when the war broke out. He had driven in the first Indianapolis 500, and had also set a speed record of 134 miles (216 km) per hour in Daytona Beach, Florida. In 1917, Eddie Rickenbacker was a sergeant in France, driving General John Pershing's staff car.

One frequent passenger was General William "Billy" Mitchell, commander of the U.S. flying corps. It was Mitchell who convinced General Pershing that Rickenbacker would be more valuable as a pilot than a chauffeur. After attending flight school, Rickenbacker became a skilled pilot and brilliant tactical fighter. He soon found himself in charge of the 94th Aero Pursuit Squadron, which was also called the Hat-in-Ring Squadron because of its distinctive insignia.

Rickenbacker was a brave pilot, but not reckless. He liked to patiently position himself above the enemy, with the sun at his back, then quickly dive down, guns blazing at the last moment. By the end of the war, Rickenbacker scored 26 victories, many against Manfred von Richthofen's Flying Circus. For his exploits in the air, Rickenbacker earned a Congressional Medal of Honor.

MANFRED VON RICHTHOFEN, GERMANY

By far the most famous and successful ace of World War I was Germany's Manfred von Richthofen. He scored 80 confirmed air victories, more than any other pilot in the war.

Above: Manfred von Richthofen.

Richthofen was born to a noble German family. His father wanted him to become an army officer, but young Manfred was more interested in horses and gymnastics. Shortly after the war began, Richthofen found himself stationed in the trenches. He managed to get a transfer to the air service, and by the end of 1915 had earned his pilot's license.

Richthofen wasn't a naturally gifted pilot, but soon learned the skills necessary for fighting in the air. Under the direction of German ace Oswald Boelcke, Richthofen quickly scored many victories. He was given command of his own squadron, Jasta 2, in January 1917. Shortly after that he commanded Jasta 11.

Richthofen's fame spread as he scored more and more victories. Many of his squadron-mates were inexperienced. So that they could more easily identify him during combat, Richthofen had his Albatros biplane painted bright red. Some said he also had the plane painted red to taunt or frighten his opponents. Allied pilots began calling Richthofen the Red Baron.

Richthofen recorded the following air battle in his logbook on April 2, 1917: "Together with Lieutenants Voss and Lothar von Richthofen, I attacked an enemy squadron of eight Sopwiths above a closed cover of clouds on the enemy's side of the lines.

Above: A German Albatros D.V, painted bright red in the style of Richthofen's plane.

"The plane I had singled out was driven away from its formation and tried to escape me by hiding in the clouds after I had put holes in its gasoline tanks.

"Below the clouds, I immediately attacked him again, thereby forcing him to land 300 yards east of Givenchy. But as yet my adversary would not surrender, and even as his machine was on the ground, he kept shooting at me, thereby hitting my machine very severely when I was only five yards off the ground.

"Consequently, I attacked him already on the ground and killed one of the occupants."

In June 1917, Richthofen headed a group of about 50 of Germany's best pilots. Officially, the group was called JG1, but it soon became known as the Flying Circus. They took off in huge V formations, with Richthofen in the lead in his red plane, striking fear into Allied pilots.

On July 6, 1917, Richthofen crashed. He survived, but suffered a severe head wound. When he returned to service, his plane had been replaced with a Fokker Dr. I triplane. The Dr. I was very maneuverable. In the hands of a skilled pilot like Richthofen, it was a deadly flying machine. By April 1918, Richthofen scored his 80th air victory, more than any other pilot.

Richthofen was killed in a dogfight on April 21, 1918, by Canadian pilot Captain Roy Brown. The Red Baron had been chasing a Sopwith Camel and didn't notice Brown's Camel trailing behind in the confusion of the dogfight. Brown fired a single burst at the red triplane, then veered off as Richthofen's plane crashed in no-man's-land.

Australian ground troops arrived at the scene of the crash and were amazed to find Richthofen's body in the wreckage, dead from a single bullet wound to the chest. There is some controversy as to whether Richthofen was struck by ground fire from the Australian troops, but credit is usually given to Brown for the victory over the Red Baron.

Richthofen was buried with full military honors the next day in Bertangles, France, by British and Australian troops. Germany mourned the loss of its famous ace.

After the war, in 1925, Richthofen's body was reburied in Berlin, Germany.

Above: Manfred von Richthoven's red Fokker Dr.I triplane. The Dr.I was difficult to fly, but very dangerous in the hands of a skilled pilot like the Red Baron.

TOP WORLD WAR I ACES
BY COUNTRY, CONFIRMED VICTORIES

COUNTRY	PILOT	VICTORIES
Germany	Manfred von Richthofen	80
France	René Fonck	75
United Kingdom	Edward Mannock	73
Canada	William Bishop	72
South Africa	A. Beauchampt-Proctor	47
Australia	Robert Little	47
Ireland	George McElroy	47
Belgium	Willy Coppens	37
Austria-Hungary	Godwin Brumowski	35
Italy	Francesco Baracca	34
USA	Eddie Rickenbacker	26
Russia	Alexei Kazakov	17

TimeLine

1914 *June 28:* Austria-Hungary's Archduke Franz Ferdinand is assassinated by a Serbian nationalist while touring Sarajevo, the capital of Bosnia-Herzegovina.

1914 *August:* World War I begins as German armed forces invade Belgium and France.

1914 *August 26-31:* Russia suffers a major defeat at the Battle of Tannenberg.

1914 *September 9-14:* Second massive Russian defeat, this time at the Battle of the Masurian Lakes.

1915 *Spring:* German Zeppelins launch bombing raids over English cities.

1915 *April 22:* Germans are first to use lethal poison gas on a large scale during the Battle of Ypres.

1915 *May:* Anthony Fokker designs synchronized machine guns for his EIII Eindecker airplane.

1915 *May 7:* A German U-boat sinks the unarmed British passenger liner *Lusitania*, killing 1,198 people, including 128 Americans. The American public is outraged, but President Wilson manages to keep the U.S. neutral.

1916 *February 21-December 18:* The Battle of Verdun. Nearly one million soldiers are killed or wounded.

1916 *June 24-November 13:* The Battle of the Somme costs approximately 1.25 million casualties. On the first day of the infantry attack, July 1, British forces suffered a staggering 60,000 casualties, including 20,000 dead, the largest single-day casualty total in British military history. Many troops are killed by a new battlefield weapon, the machine gun.

1917 *January 31:* Germany declares unrestricted submarine warfare, outraging the American public.

1917 *March 12:* The Russian Revolution overthrows Tsar Nicholas II. The country is taken over by Lenin's communist government during the Bolshevik Revolution on November 7.

1917 *April 6:* The United States declares war on Germany.

1917 *June:* Manfred von Richthofen takes command of JG1, which would become known as the Flying Circus.

1917 *December 15:* Russia's Bolshevik government agrees to a separate peace with Germany, taking Russia out of the war.

1918 *March 21-July 19:* Germany mounts five "Ludendorff offensives" against strengthening Allied forces. The attacks are costly to both sides, but Germany fails to crush the Allied armies.

1918 *April 21:* Manfred von Richthofen is shot down and killed after scoring 80 confirmed victories, more than any other pilot of World War I.

1918 *May 30-June 17:* American forces are successful against the Germans at Chateau-Thierry and Belleau Woods.

1918 *July:* British ace Edward Mannock is shot down and killed.

1918 *September 26-November 11:* French and American forces launch the successful Meuse-Argonne Offensive.

1918 *September 27-October 17:* British forces break through the Hindenburg Line.

1918 *November 11:* Armistice Day. Fighting stops at 11:00 A.M.

1919 *May 7-June 28:* The Treaty of Versailles is written and signed.

GLOSSARY

ALLIES
In World War I, the countries fighting against the Central Powers: Great Britain, France, Russia, and to a small extent, Japan. Italy joined the Allies in 1916, and the United States joined in 1917. Also in 1917, Russia dropped out of the war.

ATTRITION
A gradual process of weakening or wearing down. World War I is often referred to as a war of attrition, because each side hoped to win by causing unacceptably high casualties to the enemy. At the Battle of Verdun, the Germans planned to "bleed France white" by throwing wave after wave of attackers against French strongholds. The French suffered very high numbers of casualties, but so did the Germans, who were eventually forced to call off the attacks.

BIPLANE
A plane that has two sets of wings, one on top of the other. This was a common design of airplanes in World War I.

CASUALTY
Soldiers killed or wounded in battle.

CENTRAL POWERS
In World War I, the countries fighting against the Allies: Germany, Austria-Hungary, Turkey, and Bulgaria.

CONGRESSIONAL MEDAL OF HONOR
The U.S. military's highest decoration, awarded by Congress for "gallantry at the risk of life above and beyond the call of duty."

DOGFIGHT
Air-to-air combat between opposing sides of aircraft.

FUSELAGE
The main body of an airplane, not including the wings, tail, or engine.

INCENDIARY BULLETS
Bullets that are designed to start fires on impact. They are often loaded with flammable material, like phosphorous. Airplanes often used incendiary bullets against Zeppelins in order to set them on fire and force them down.

MONOPLANE
A plane with a single set of wings. The Fokker EIII Eindecker is an example of a monoplane.

NEUTRAL COUNTRY
A country that doesn't participate in a war between other countries. Sometimes neutral countries bend the definition of the word. Even though the United States stayed neutral until 1917, it actively traded goods and weapons with both sides, although it had especially close economic ties with the Allied countries.

NO-MAN'S-LAND
The area of land between two opposing lines of trenches.

POSTHUMOUS
Arising or continuing after one's death. In the military, to be awarded a medal posthumously means to be honored after death.

RECONNAISSANCE
To explore or scout the enemy's position. Aircraft in World War I were very useful in discovering the enemy's exact location, which helped make artillery fire more accurate. As both sides began to realize the importance of aerial reconnaissance, they each developed fighter aircraft to shoot down enemy reconnaissance planes.

TRIPLANE
A plane that has three sets of wings stacked on top of each other. At one point in his career Manfred von Richthofen flew a bright red Fokker Dr. I triplane.

WEB SITES

Would you like to learn more about the airplanes of World War I? Please visit **www.abdopub.com** to find up-to-date Web site links. These links are routinely monitored and updated to provide the most current information available.

INDEX